BLAZERS

ALL ABOUT FANTASY CREATURES

Discover DRAGONS, GIANTS

AND Other Deadly Fantasy Monsters

A.J. Sautter

Raintree

company — publishers for children

Raintree is an imprint of Capstone Global Library Limited, a company incorporated in England and Wales having its registered office at 264 Banbury Road, Oxford, OX2 7DY – Registered company number: 6695582

www.raintree.co.uk
myorders@raintree.co.uk

Edited by Adrian Vigliano
Designed by Bobbie Nuytten
Picture research by Wanda Winch
Production by Laura Manthe
Originated by Capstone Global Library
Printed and bound in China

ISBN 978 1 4747 4258 0
21 20 19 18 17
10 9 8 7 6 5 4 3 2 1

British Library Cataloguing in Publication Data
A full catalogue record for this book is available from the British Library.

Acknowledgements
We would like to thank the following for permission to reproduce photographs: Capstone: Colin Ashcroft, 21, 32, Collin Howard, 7, 9, Jason Juta, 4, 15, 27, Martin Bustamante, cover (bottom left), 1 (left), 5, 17, Stefano Azzalin, 23, Tom McGrath, cover (top right), 11, 13, 19; Dreamstime: Chorazin3d, 28 (bottom); Shutterstock: BergelmLicht, cover (background), 1 (background), Firstear, 25, Marafona, 9 (background), Valentyna Chukhlyebova, 3, 28 (top)

Every effort has been made to contact copyright holders of material reproduced in this book. Any omissions will be rectified in subsequent printings if notice is given to the publisher.

CONTENTS

DEADLY FANTASY MONSTERS!

Fantasy tales are full of deadly monsters. Dragons attack villages to steal treasure. Giants, ogres and trolls like to **ambush** unwitting travellers. What would these monsters do if they were real? Where would they live? What would they eat? Turn the page and find out!

> **ambush** make a surprise attack

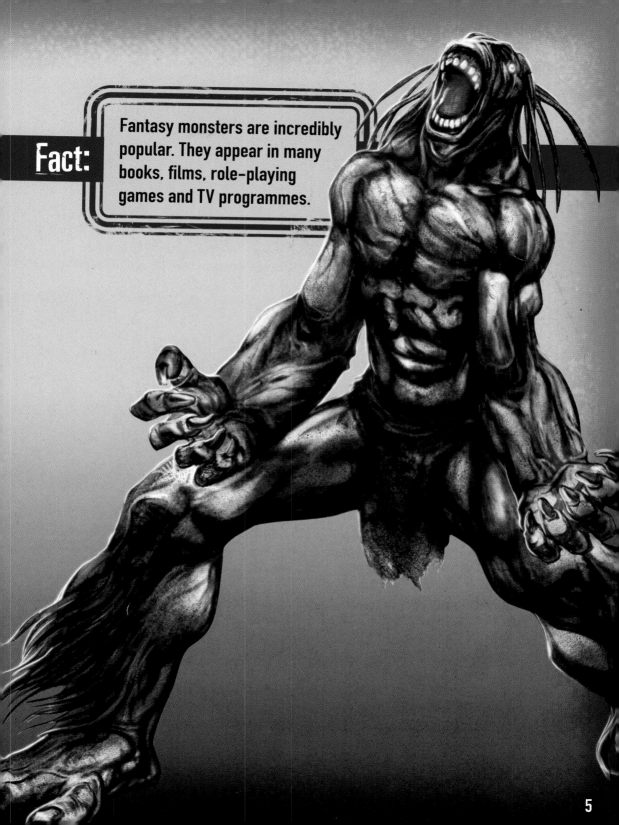

Fact: Fantasy monsters are incredibly popular. They appear in many books, films, role-playing games and TV programmes.

BLACK DRAGONS

Size: 37 metres (120 ft) long;
wingspans up to 46 metres (150 ft)

Home: caves with hidden entrances found
in **bogs** or swamps

Diet: turtles, alligators, opossums, muskrats, humans

Lifespan: up to 2,200 years

Appearance: Black dragons have thin, bony bodies. They often have diseased skin and tattered wings. Like most dragons, black dragons have deadly teeth, claws and tails. They also have deadly acid breath that can dissolve the thickest armour.

bog area of wet, spongy land, often filled with dead and rotting plants

Behaviour: Black dragons are vicious and cruel. They enjoy causing pain in others. They also like to collect treasure. They like gold coins more than gems or other valuables.

EASTERN DRAGONS

Size: more than 61 metres (200 ft) long

Home: caves found near rivers and lakes

Diet: fish, deer, sheep, rabbits, squirrels

Lifespan: more than 8,000 years

Appearance: Eastern dragons are brightly coloured with red, yellow, blue or green scales. Their bodies are similar to huge snakes. Most have antlers like a deer. Their four feet are tipped with sharp **talons**. Eastern dragons don't have wings. However, they can use magic to soar through the air.

talon long, sharp claw

drought long period of weather with little or no rainfall

Behaviour: Eastern dragons can be deadly, but they are often helpful towards humans. Some have used magic to bring rain and end **droughts**. Eastern dragons enjoy collecting gems such as rubies and emeralds.

Red Dragons

Size: 46 metres (150 ft) long;
wingspans up to 55 metres (180 ft)

Home: **lairs** found in deep caves in large mountains

Diet: deer, sheep, cattle, humans

Lifespan: more than 2,500 years

Appearance: Red dragons usually have dark red or red-gold scales. They have four legs and huge leathery wings. Their weapons include razor-sharp claws, wicked teeth and powerful whip-like tails.

lair place where a wild animal lives and sleeps

hoard money, gold or other valuables that are stored or hidden away

Behaviour: Red dragons gain their treasure by stealing it. They fiercely protect their treasure **hoards**. If someone tries to steal a single coin, they'll blast the person with their fiery breath.

White Dragons

Size: 31 metres (100 ft) long;
    wingspans up to 37 metres (120 ft)

Home: icy caves on tall mountain peaks or large icebergs

Diet: fish, walruses, elk, small whales

Lifespan: up to 2,000 years

Appearance: White dragons have white or light blue scales. A bony **frill** helps to protect their necks. They have two legs, two large wings, sharp claws and teeth, and powerful tails.

frill bony collar that fans out around an animal's neck

grudge feeling of anger towards someone who has hurt or insulted you in the past

Behaviour: White dragons love treasure, but they like diamonds and silver coins best. They use their icy breath for defence and hunting prey. Ice dragons have long memories. If insulted, they'll hold onto a **grudge** for hundreds of years.

CYCLOPS

Size: about 4.6 metres (15 ft) tall

Home: mountain caves or ruined castles

Diet: sheep, goats, deer, rabbits, squirrels

Lifespan: 450 to 500 years

Appearance: Cyclops have stocky bodies and strong hands. Most don't have hair, but a few have bushy beards. Cyclops are best known for their single large eye. Looking into a Cyclops' eye can cause paralysing fear in a person.

blacksmith someone who makes and fixes things made of iron or steel

forge special furnace in which metal is heated

Behaviour: Most Cyclops live alone. They spend their days protecting their animals and homes from intruders. Some are skilled **blacksmiths**. They create magical weapons and armour in their secret **forges**.

Ettins

Size: 6 to 7.6 metres (20 to 25 ft) tall
Home: underground caves found in rocky hills
Diet: deer, elk, sheep, goats, humans
Lifespan: 90 to 100 years

Appearance: Ettins have muscular bodies and two or more heads. Each head controls a different part of the body. Ettins never bathe. They usually stink of sweat and rotting food.

Behaviour: Ettins will eat any meat they can catch, including humans. They live alone and don't like to be disturbed. Ettins aren't very clever. However, they are skilled fighters with their spiked clubs.

Mountain giants

Size: more than 13 metres (45 ft) tall
Home: large caves in mountains or hidden valleys
Diet: deer, elk, sheep, goats, humans
Lifespan: 600 to 700 years

Appearance: Mountain giants look like huge human beings. However, their tough skin is usually a stony grey colour. They have black, brown or fiery red hair. Most males have huge, bushy beards.

Behaviour: Mountain giants like to be left alone. If disturbed, they will smash outsiders with their huge clubs. Mountain giants often enjoy rock battles. They hurl huge boulders at one another high up in the mountains.

OGRES

Size: 2.4 to 3 metres (8 to 10 ft) tall

Home: damp caves near mountains or stinking swamps

Diet: snakes, snails, slugs, grubs, humans

Lifespan: about 50 years

Appearance: Ogres are amazingly strong. Their tough skin is often green in colour. Many ogres have **deformities** such as club hands or hunched backs. Some have sharp tusks in their bottom jaws.

deformity being twisted, bent or disfigured in some way

raid sudden, surprise attack on a place

Behaviour: Ogres hate the sun and avoid sunlight whenever possible. Ogres are usually violent and cruel. They enjoy hurting their enemies and hearing them cry out in pain. Ogres have few skills. They often **raid** nearby villages to steal what they need.

CAVE TROLLS

Size: 3 to 3.7 metres (10 to 12 ft) tall
Home: deep, dark mountain caves
Diet: sheep, deer, horses, dwarves, humans
Lifespan: 65 to 75 years

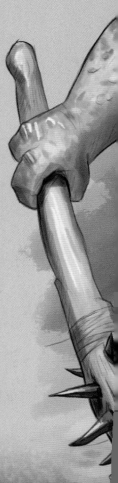

Appearance: Cave trolls have long arms and huge, muscular bodies. Their rough skin often looks like stone. They have sharp, jagged teeth and two large tusks. They often stand hunched over in an ape-like **stance**.

> **stance** position of someone's arms, legs and body

Behaviour: Cave trolls are active only at night. If exposed to sunlight, they turn into solid stone. Cave trolls often work with orcs to ambush travellers. Sometimes they steal animals to eat from nearby farms.

FOREST TROLLS

Size: 3.7 to 4.6 metres (12 to 15 ft) tall

Home: dark caves hidden in thick forests

Diet: any kind of animal, dwarves, humans

Lifespan: about 200 years

Appearance: Forest trolls have green skin. Their huge bodies are usually covered in thick brown hair. Their mouths are full of jagged, rotten teeth. Large tusks jut out from their lower jaws.

intelligence ability to learn and understand information

Behaviour: Forest trolls are rarely seen. They will fiercely attack anyone who wanders into their territory. Most trolls have little **intelligence**. Some forest trolls know how to make and use simple armour and weapons.

SWAMP TROLLS

Size: 2.4 to 3 metres (8 to 10 ft) tall
Home: tropical swamps and bogs
Diet: fish, frogs, snakes, muskrats, alligators, humans
Lifespan: 90 to 100 years

Appearance:
Swamp trolls have dark green or black skin. Swamp trolls' large hands are tipped with wicked claws. Their mouths are filled with sharp, jagged teeth. Their bodies heal quickly from wounds. Only fire or acid can kill and destroy a swamp troll.

Behaviour:
Swamp trolls are savage and violent. They attack humans and other creatures on sight. Swamp trolls hate sunlight and are active only at night.

Creature quiz

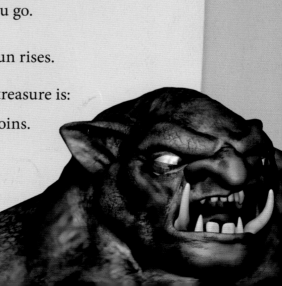

1. Ogres raid villages at night to:

   A) steal food and supplies.
   B) avoid sunlight.
   C) both A and B.

2. Red dragons usually live in:

   A) stinking bogs and swamps.
   B) deep caves in the mountains.
   C) large castles or forts.

3. Ettins have more than one head. They usually tend to:

   A) be very intelligent.
   B) be skilled fighters.
   C) argue with themselves.

4. If a cave troll catches you, you should:

   A) try to convince him to let you go.
   B) fight your way past him.
   C) keep him talking until the sun rises.

5. An Eastern dragon's favourite treasure is:

   A) shiny diamonds and silver coins.
   B) colourful jewels and gems.
   C) golden coins.

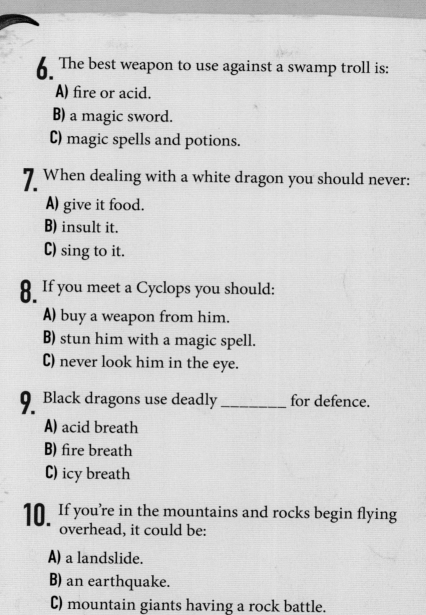

6. The best weapon to use against a swamp troll is:

   A) fire or acid.

   B) a magic sword.

   C) magic spells and potions.

7. When dealing with a white dragon you should never:

   A) give it food.

   B) insult it.

   C) sing to it.

8. If you meet a Cyclops you should:

   A) buy a weapon from him.

   B) stun him with a magic spell.

   C) never look him in the eye.

9. Black dragons use deadly _____ for defence.

   A) acid breath

   B) fire breath

   C) icy breath

10. If you're in the mountains and rocks begin flying overhead, it could be:

   A) a landslide.

   B) an earthquake.

   C) mountain giants having a rock battle.

See page 31 for quiz answers.

Glossary

ambush   make a surprise attack

blacksmith   someone who makes and fixes things made of iron or steel

bog   area of wet, spongy land, often filled with dead and rotting plants

deformity   being twisted, bent or disfigured in some way

drought   long period of weather with little or no rainfall

forge   special furnace in which metal is heated

frill   bony collar that fans out around an animal's neck

grudge   feeling of anger towards someone who has hurt or insulted you in the past

hoard   money, gold or other valuables that are stored or hidden away

intelligence   ability to learn and understand information

lair   place where a wild animal lives and sleeps

raid   sudden, surprise attack on a place

stance   position of someone's arms, legs and body

talon   long, sharp claw

Find out more
Books

The Anatomy of a Dragon (The World of Dragons),
Matt Doeden (Raintree, 2013)

How to Draw Fantasy Creatures, Paul Bryn Davies and
Jim McCarthy (Search Press, 2015)

Tell Me a Dragon, Jackie Morris (Frances Lincoln
Children's Books, 2016)

Quiz answers:
1:C, 2:B, 3:B, 4:C, 5:B, 6:A, 7:B, 8:C, 9:A, 10:C

Websites

**www.dkfindout.com/uk/explore/how-to-spot-dragon-
five-dragons-from-around-world**
Myths about dragons are told all over the world. Find out
more on this web page.

**www.dkfindout.com/uk/explore/tall-stories-were-
giants-real**
Read this web page to find out more about giants.

www.howtotrainyourdragonbooks.com
Find out about the *How to Train Your Dragon* books.

Index

Discover DRAGONS, GIANTS

and Other Deadly Fantasy Monsters

What kind of weapons do dragons use? How do most giants like to live? What is the best defence against ogres and trolls? Do you know what to do if you met one of these dangerous creatures in person? Learn all about these deadly fantasy monsters and more inside.

ALL ABOUT FANTASY CREATURES

Have you ever wanted to see a dragon, elf or unicorn in person? Creatures like these live only in people's imaginations. But what if they actually existed? Here's your chance to learn about your favourite fantastic creatures and how they'd live in the world if they were real.

TITLES IN THIS SERIES

Discover Dragons, Giants
and Other Deadly Fantasy Monsters

Discover Gnomes, Halflings
and Other Wondrous Fantasy Beings

Discover Harpies, Minotaurs
and Other Mythical Fantasy Beasts

Discover Orcs, Boggarts
and Other Nasty Fantasy Creatures

Book Band Level: Brown

ISBN 978-1-4747-4258-0

9 781474 742580

raintree
a Capstone company—publishers for children
www.raintree.co.uk